Easter 2023

This book belongs to:

My Beautiful Grandchildren:
Nicole and Elisa

With all my love, your
grandmother "Gawa"

God Hears When You Pray

Originally published by iCharacter as two separate books under the titles
Psalm 34 and The Lord's Prayer.
Published by arrangement with iCharacter Limited (Ireland).
www.iCharacter.org

Published by Christian Art Kids, an imprint of Christian Art Publishers,
PO Box 1599, Vereeniging, 1930, RSA

© 2019
First edition 2019

Illustrated by Agnes de Bezenac

Scripture quotations are taken from the *Holy Bible*, New Living Translation®, copyright © 1996, 2004, 2007, 2013, 2015 by Tyndale House Foundation. Used by permission of Tyndale House Publishers, Inc., Carol Stream, Illinois 60188. All rights reserved.

Scripture quotations are taken from the New King James Version. Copyright © 1979, 1980, 1982 by Thomas Nelson, Inc. Used by permission. All rights reserved.

Printed in China

ISBN 978-1-4321-2938-5

22 23 24 25 26 27 28 29 30 31 – 14 13 12 11 10 9 8 7 6 5

Printed in Shenzhen, China
JULY 2022
Print Run: PUR402509

GOD HEARS
WHEN YOU PRAY

christian art kids

I will always say good things about God, and talk about how great He is.

I will praise the Lord at all times. I will constantly speak His praises.

(Psalm 34:1)

When I'm feeling down,
I know God's power
can help me feel stronger.

I will boast only in the Lord;
let all who are helpless
take heart.

(Psalm 34:2)

Let's worship God together, and talk about how wonderful He is.

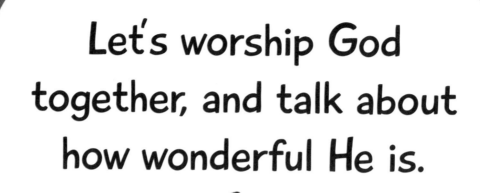

Come, let us tell of
the Lord's greatness;
let us exalt His name together.

(Psalm 34:3)

When I pray to God,
He hears me and I
no longer feel afraid.

I prayed to the Lord,
and He answered me.
He freed me from all my fears.

(Psalm 34:4)

When God
is in my life,
I feel proud of myself.

Those who look to Him for
help will be radiant with
joy; no shadow of shame
will darken their faces.

(Psalm 34:5)

13

When I have problems,
I can pray,
and God will help me.

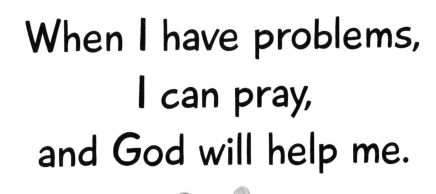

In my desperation I prayed,
and the Lord listened; He saved
me from all my troubles.

(Psalm 34:6)

God's angels
are all around me,
and they protect me.

For the angel of the Lord
is a guard; He surrounds
and defends all
who fear Him.

(Psalm 34:7)

All my senses tell me
that God is good and
will watch over me.

Taste and see that the Lord
is good. Oh, the joys of those
who take refuge in Him!

(Psalm 34:8)

I respect
God, so He takes
excellent care of me.

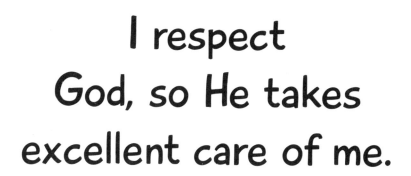

Fear the Lord, you His godly
people, for those who fear
Him will have all they need.

(Psalm 34:9)

Even strong animals sometimes go hungry, but those who pray to God will always have what they need.

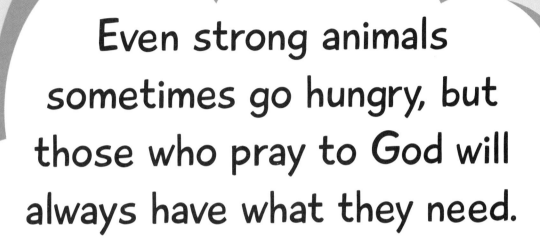

Even strong young lions sometimes go hungry, but those who trust in the Lord will lack no good thing.

(Psalm 34:10)

I love to
read the Bible.
It teaches me how
I can worship God.

Come, my children,
and listen to me,
and I will teach you
to fear the Lord.

(Psalm 34:11)

I want my days to be happy,
so I try not to speak
bad about others.
And always tell the truth.

Does anyone want to live a life
that is long and prosperous?
Then keep your tongue from speaking
evil and your lips from telling lies!

(Psalm 34:12-13)

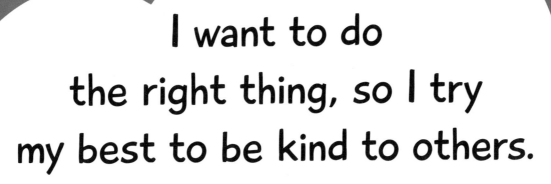

I want to do
the right thing, so I try
my best to be kind to others.

Turn away from evil and do good.
Search for peace,
and work to maintain it.

(Psalm 34:14)

God keeps His eye
on me, and is there
when I need Him.

The eyes of the Lord watch
over those who do right;
His ears are open to their
cries for help.

(Psalm 34:15)

"Our Father in heaven,"

Matthew 6:9

We are praying
to God.
He is our loving
father in heaven.

"Hallowed be Your name."

Matthew 6:9

Hallowed means "holy"
or "great." It's like saying,
"Your name is awesome!"

"Your kingdom come."

Matthew 6:10

God's kingdom is a loving place to be.

"Your will be done
on earth as it is in heaven."

Matthew 6:10

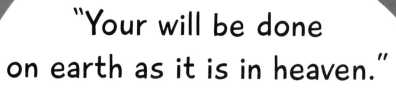

God wants us to live in
peace and with goodness,
so that earth will
be like heaven.

"Give us this day
our daily bread."

Matthew 6:11

We trust God to
give us what
we need every day.

"And forgive us our debts,
as we forgive our debtors."

Matthew 6:12

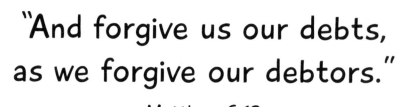

We're asking God to
forgive us for our mistakes,
and we promise to forgive
people who have
done wrong to us.

"And do not lead us into temptation,
but deliver us from the evil one."

Matthew 6:13

We're asking God to help
us do the right thing,
even when that's hard.

"For Yours is
the kingdom and the power
and the glory forever."

Matthew 6:13

God is wonderful and
powerful, and will
stay that way
forever.

"Amen."

Amen means
"so be it," or
"this is the truth
and I agree."